OF TYRANT

Also by Leah Umansky:

Domestic Uncertainties
The Barbarous Century
Don Dreams and I Dream
Straight Away the Emptied World

OF TYRANT

Leah Umansky

THE WORD WORKS
WASHINGTON, D.C.

THE WORD WORKS

P.O. Box 42164
Washington, DC 20015
editor@wordworksbooks.org
Author photograph:
Interior design: Emma Berver
Cover design: Susan Pearce
Cover art: Collage by Leah Umansky

ISBN: 978-1-944585-74-7
LCCN: 2024930175

ACKNOWLEDGMENTS

Thank you to the editors of these journals where these poems or versions were originally published, some with different titles. Thank you for all you do for poetry and for saying YES to these poems.

American Poetry Review: "I Want to Wear the Crown" & "What Does the X Mark"
Cincinnati Review: "Tender" & "God Is God and the Universe Is the Universe"
Ep;phany: "[of men]"
Forklift, Ohio: "[of] Tyrant in Jest"
Glass Poetry Journal: "Of Tyrant" & "Alternate Ending of the Tyrant"
Golden Walkman: "Anarchy City"
Love's Executive Order: "Evolution Hinges on Its Mistake," What Even Matters Anymore," & "The Other Side of Hatred"
Minyan Magazine: "Stun"
Missouri Review: "Rise and Fall of the Tyrant"
North American Review "What You Give to a Thief Is Stolen"
On the Seawall: "Make It"
Painted Bride Quarterly: "Woman Alive"
Pleiades: "Marvel [at Woman] or Woman: Last Monster"
Plume Anthology 8: "Torpor"
The Academy of American Poets' *Poem-a-Day*: "Desire [even in the time of the tyrant]"
Poetry City: "What They Recognize is the Smell"
Poetry International: "Self-Reflection"
Rhino: "Tyrant as Self-Reflection"
Salamander: "Hate Dream"
Shrew Literary Zine: "Stay Quiet"
The White Review: "Stone," and "Gasp"

Thank you to my mom, Ronnie Umansky, who always told me I should write political poems and taught me that each of us is political, to my dad, Arthur Umansky, to my sister, Faith Umansky, and to Scott Walsh.

Additional thanks to the following people for their support, friendship and community: Kaveh Akbar, Hala Alyan, Virginia Bell, Patricia Carlin, Laura Cronk, Kelly Davio, Sarah Davis, Marcy Dermansky, Dante and Christina Di Stefano, Joseph Duane, Jenny Franklin, Melissa Fite

Johnson, Sammy Greenspan, Adam J. Gellings, Sarah Gerard, David Gutowski, Dena Rash Guzman, Ilya Kaminsky, Damien Kempf, Virginia Konchan, Paige Lewis, Kathryn Maris, Nathan McClain, Heather Marshall, Niall Munro, Faisal Mohyuddin, Ellen and Drew Paulik, Robert Polito, Louise Rodwell and family, Lori Schwarz, Diane Seuss, Don Share, Tara Skurtu, Jacob Steingroot, Hannah Stephenson, Jill Sullivan, KC Trommer, Barbara Louise Ungar, Donna Vorreyer, and Devon Walker-Figuora.

Additional thanks to everyone in our 15+ year Carlin Workshop—you guys are always the best part of my week: Susan Bruce, Bergen Hutaff, Sarah Paley, Heather Newman, W.R. Weinstein, Suze Bienaimee, and Beth Dufford.

And to my editor, Nancy White, for always fighting for this book, even from the start. You inspire me. Thank you for your efforts, your friendship and your sense of humor. Sometimes all we can do in this world is laugh.

CONTENTS

In a dark time, the eye begins to see.

—Theodore Roethke

'Twas yet some comfort when misery could beguile
the tyrant's rage and frustrate his proud will.

—William Shakespeare, *King Lear*

Who knows what they say or where they are likely to go?
Who can tell what they really are? Under their daily-ness.

—Margaret Atwood, *The Handmaid's Tale*

TWO LIVES

Let's start with the child and use that darling as a device.
A little chaos makes a good story. When it comes to tormented goodness,

Look around. On the F train, I saw a mother and her child lock eyes.
The child pushed through the crowd, her mouth—a harsh parallel,

Her eyes—a controlled earthquake of dread, of fragmented haunting,
Of dense, hard grey stone. Through the rush-hour crowd, she pushed,

As in a solitary migration to her mother, to the door, in an orb of her own,
But I couldn't hear her words. I only heard the mother, preening, leaning-in

Teaching her daughter to grasp her strength, to clench her fist,
To rise against the spasm of silence. No one could hear the girl

But I saw her push. I saw her strive. Her silence wasn't learned,
Or practiced, just fell upon, like so much in this life. The mother,

Riddled in grocery bags, errands, sweat and homework, grabbed
Her daughter's delicate wrist, her breath stood on her chin, her eyes bore

Into her, in nightmare. I felt the invisible line of pain forming around that
Wrist, like a system of star-like bruises, but there were no visible marks.

She said, "Use your words, honey. You've got to use your words."
And in that fog of must, I saw a life outside of this one. A life where daughters

Don't need such lessons. A seemingly-un-brutal future held up by all of us.
Such lessons would fall away, an escapable pattern of a life gone astray.

If you weren't paying attention, you might've said *villain,*
Thief, Tyrant, but the word, *truth-teller* came to my lips.

The rage of that mother, to get her daughter to speak,
To get her daughter to speak loudly, to get her daughter to speak up

Like a boy or a man. Teach the girl what must become innate
And exile forever the faults of this world. Start with what the Tyrant

Loves to throw: his words, his voice, his weight.

WHAT DOES THE X MARK?

There are dancers on the train, boys, teenagers, contorting their bodies through the slither of the subway. The spool of the stop and go, the rush of the slide, the stir, the silence, the whir. The dancers look at a woman, her body, an X of bone and bone, her body, a warning, a stop, a flare. She screams: *i just want to be left alone i just want to be left alone i just want to be left alone* and the dancers say, *dancing isn't criminal; don't take your bad day out on us.*

*

In the Lyft, going to the airport, a 90-year-old retired man, our driver Mario and I start talking about driving. The old man says that he gave up his license years ago, that he doesn't want to be responsible for taking anyone's life but is fine with someone taking his own.

Mario and I look at each other in the rearview.

Mario says, *no, no, every one of us is important.*

*

On the train in Chicago, after leaving the conservatory, I sit on the train, riding into the Loop, a peel of the city, a circle, a circuit, a turn gone wrong then right; two couples get on and sit opposite me; I am reading a book; lost in the page and the word and the desire of Elio and Oliver. I look up from the felt-life to my real life and see both women opposite me have their right legs crossed over the right leg of their partners, their men; It is like an abstraction, a surrealist painting, a beyond I can't reach; I stare at these circuits of power and play, of desire and play, of power and crosshairs (and god, it *felt* like a warning) and I sat there feeling disgust and something sallow and a felt a circle had formed around me, and suddenly in the silent chaos, in the temptation that wasn't there, I felt a thirst (was it jealousy, envy, longing?) I don't know, but I felt elongated, inside the circumference; arc-ed, radiant;

I felt punctured yet punctual, red and fired, scalding, and scarleted, yet bound; where was the mark, where was the marker, and had the X already been drawn?

*

I was alone and alone I was and I got off at my stop and went beyond the surface, underground, to the subway where a woman was holding a baby, dancing, orbiting closer and closer to the performer singing on the platform, *at last my love has come along; my lonely days are over and life is like a song* and I stand there, looking for the song and the love and what lies outside our power; outside the woman; outside the people that protect themselves from their selves.

*

Every one of us important

OF TYRANT

We are made to persist. That is how we know who we are.
                 —a fortune cookie

1.

I fetch the rage.

2.

I fetch the rage
        in chaos,
in the heel of
        this butchering,
in the squeezing
        of the heart.

listening
        (or not)
to his word
to his garbage
it is all lies

I won't.

3.

he is an open fire

4.

the anger unsettles
the heart
turns to
to   to
        to cowering
to fowl
to flight
into air
into glass
blasts
        us all
into slick
into sick
into darkness

5.

who needs loyalty
when all is pounded
        into fatigue.
I cannot reiterate this enough:

the past
isn't dead.
embrace
these rough edges
the corrosive doors
the tipping of lies
the tangle of webs
or thorns
or tweets
I can't

6.

Jimmy Kimmel says
it is like someone
has opened a window
to hell.
I
I
I
I
can't sink this rage
it stills
it stills
it stills itself into flame
I
can't watch the news anymore
I
can barely stay positive
not now
not now
not now
(he can't make me say,
                    never)
never you mind
the rise to rage
is not of fury
but of tyrant
of tyrant

7.

I will turn
I will turn my gaze
away from the flames
I will turn my gaze
upward
skybound
& wide

8.

gather

gather your good
gather your good appetite

gather
your filling

gather
your filling of

hate

I WANT TO WEAR THE CROWN

A teacher at school tells me *the Constitution starts with the people and ends with the people*. He says, *the Constitution protects the people against tyranny*, and I think, *what protects the people from the people? What protects the people from their selves?*

*

My horoscope tells me the year ahead is my emerald year and that I'm going to wear the crown

*

The other day, I overheard my friend say to her dog, *how do you live with someone so miserable?*

*

Every one of us is important, and I *want* to wear the crown; I want to mind the brilliant exception that the regard with which I give myself to others, is not shortchanged; is not a testament to sorrow or to slight, but an endless attraction to everything and nothing; who doesn't know the capacity of their heart; its limits; the grace with which it exhausts in on itself; as an accordion, the sureness of its belief; its because and its inhibitions

*

It loved me and it loved me, and it loved me and therefore the very definition of the self was behind, but forward; a despair of connection, an exile of the piecing of time

therefore therefore therefore therefore

STONE

Stone heart. Stone deep. Stone minded. Turn to Stone. Stoned. Stone. I turn to stone when I'm argumentative. I turn to stone when I turn chaotic. My chaos is a bag of stones. I turn to stone when he is on fire. I will coat this in stones. I turn.

I stone.   I roll my stone.   I palm my stone.   I serve my stone.

The stage has been set. This set has been staged. This set has been stoned by the stony-hearted. I am of the stony-hearted. I am heart-stone. I think the words I am looking for are 'spite' and 'malice.' No, you are stone-cold. You are the breaker of stones. You, stonecutter. You cut the head of my stone, but not my heart. Try to touch this. Touchstone. Touch the touchstone of my want.

Of my feast   Of my safety   Of my dark   Of my light   Of my truth

Of my false   Of my fierce   Of my salt   Of my sweet.

Your slaughter is in flame and slaughter is close to water, is close to laughter, is close to aught. I *ought* to be real here. I ought to think again. I ought to stammer this home in stones. Splint in stones. Sprint in stones. Glint in stones, but not gravel, not grovel. Not pebbled in fear. Here's an interesting question. I mean the universe of language is designed to be a stone's throw from possible, right? A stone's throw from able. Wait. Didn't Abel stone Cain? They were family. They were blood. Use your words. Keep your heart stony. Create a mouth from your eye, an eye from your mouth. Use your stone heart as a harness. Use your eye as a hand. All of you will have to leave something to someone.

BURN

so this
is what it is like
to live
in the dark
where hate
is the only fuel
to light the darkness
the darkness
which darkens
its dark
with hate
the darkness
which is
darkening now
it is unbearable
to not see
the way it jags
its mouth
spitting
its tar.
no
starry night
no
beacon of light
no
no
no
no
this
pin
is stuck
in the root
of my hope
this
storm
of coal

blacks out
the sun
this
seed
of hate
shreds
the radiant
shreds
the joy
this
is what
hatred is
its greed
seething
for us
all

GOD IS GOD AND THE UNIVERSE IS THE UNIVERSE

and maybe they've had enough
and maybe the ship will finally sink
and maybe the controversy will be settled
and maybe the rendering will be palpable
and maybe the reckoning will be glorious
and maybe the divide will be bridged with glory
and maybe the flashes will be fragments
and maybe the center will not hold
and maybe the thrill of what follows will be just that: thrilling
and maybe I will see through the darkness
and maybe I will come before the remembering and see the truth
and maybe I will imagine the very heart of this moment and not feel pain
and maybe I will make a case for jealousy—that it was mine all this time
and maybe I will see my limitations as a mirror in search for a face
and maybe I will recognize the swallowing of strength
and maybe I will have intentions I didn't know I had
and maybe I will search the model I hold for splinters and cracks
and maybe my predictions were wrong
and maybe my patience didn't thin
and maybe I will have had enough
and maybe I will erase what has plagued me
and maybe the reckoning will be deafening
and maybe I will rise up
and see with these eyes that want
and these eyes that hold
and these eyes that carry
and these eyes that cast
and these eyes that glare
and maybe I will see with these eyes
that this country is good
that people are good
that people are *mostly* good
and that I knew the whole time
that I was good

WHAT THEY RECOGNIZE IS THE SMELL

At the Golden Globes, Guillermo del Toro says *he has always been faithful to monsters.* What I want to say is that I have, too: the brute, the drama, the dark side of the heart. But now, they Seem too real. The monsters in our lives are full-hearted with want and desire. Recognize Them. They are among us. Some are in charge. I turn green at the thought, khakied, lemoned. Is It true that a force lies in us? Are we triggered by a safer speaking? No, don't fortress this. The Goatish attempt must be swayed. Lament, but jade yourself forward. Lift the chin, smell.

THE OTHER SIDE OF HATRED

is innocence & good
reset is a point of *enough*
a fault of fallible.
This armor
is a doorway
of darkness
holding back
light
is a lick
away
from logic
a loneliness
farther & deeper
than a startle
i am startled
i am spun
& startling

//

you thief
you liar
you sheep
you hedge of darkness
the sting is in your haze
your gaze
your contemptible rage

you foul
you sty
you splint
its design
its eyeless child
give me that hope

///

i will fill it with more
light
good
peace
story
sisterhood

reset

reset

reset

reset

reset

reset

reset

reset

then, love

[OF MEN]

and why is it that everything is built
for the hands [of men] and why is so
much of today islanding away from us
and where is the past when we need
it and where is the love and where is
the following of one joy to the next
and where are the consequences and
repercussions and where is the captive
and where is the blued

The other day, the tyrant said, *hate
has no place in our country*, while
naming the wrong city where the
tragedy occurred, and I thought:
Is man no more than this. This
fool. This folly. This fool. This
laugh. This dance of absurdity. The
foolery [of men] and this world and
the hands of the hands [of men]

Everything moves too fast and it is
hard to live hard to insist on living
directly heart to head, heart to
mouth, heart to hand to hand to hand
and hard to insist on the gut, its taste
and reflection and what is causal and
what is pleasure and what is fleeting
and what stays behind and what is
the tempering and the patience the
politics the grappling. We cringe in
this world [of men] and shouldn't i
listen and shouldn't i be and shouldn't
i whether and shouldn't i hush and
shouldn't i know and shouldn't i
wonder declutter sit still come reveal
suggest sit still stiller still

No,

This world [of men] this world
this world this world [of men] is
merely a mention, here, this room,
this hand of my touch, take that
tyranny back. The world [of men],
their hands and hearts and hands
built for touch the world [of men]
is measly, the world [of men] is
mere mania, mere menace and
menial and measurable; this world
[of men] is merely menstrual in
rush in flow and don't they know
it? See the handling clearer. This
world is built for no one. This
world reveals another, a gentler
world with gentler hands to
hold the world [of men]; *bid the
dishonest man mend himself mend*
yourself, mend the world [of men]

GASP

Step into
This suffering
It is a stroke away from
Light
It is a stroke away from
Horror
This claim
Is a forward regime.
Step into
This smoldering.
Step into
The smolder.
Carry
Relief.
Carry
Resistance.
Carry
Tragedy.
Carry
This tragedy.
Step into
The gash
Step into
His hubris
This is not a choir.
I will not sing.

Step into

The masses.

Hear them.

At one point,

The fall

From fear

Felt terrific

But terror

Is akin to grace.

Both leave

Us gasping.

Now

We police.

Now

We lure ourselves

To fight.

To resist.

To chant.

I said

I wouldn't sing

But I do,

Inside.

Inside,

My gasp

Is an idealized prayer

I don't know what my gasp does.

I feel
Exiled.
In dream,
Exiled.
In hate,
Exiled.
In polarity
& returned
To the past.
I feel a part
Of the generous
Now gone.
But my spark
Is generous
It is a way.
It is a way
But also
Light-years ahead.
And still,
We could go up in
Smoke.
Swallowed
In horror.
In revolution.
In revolt.
We dilemma.
We plea.

It is not a wronged way, but

Step into

His famine.

Step into

His heart.

It is a step away

From murder.

All that gasping is for the ministry.

[Why is this feed so powerful?]

Use these gasps

As vows,

Except,

When we can't.

This step

Is a root

This step

Is a purge

This step

Is a struggle of ends.

Justify the means.

His heart,

Is a dull stud,

Is in my study,

Is a study away from

Tyranny.

I am putting this in the center.

[I am not even sure if you're afraid]

ANARCHY CITY

and you will lose again, he says and you will lose again and you will lose you will lose. The anarchy of the city is the anarchy of the heart broken and broke and broken-in on and upon. The anarchy of the city is in anarchy of the lies is the anarchy of unrest of rest of distress and you will lose again, he says and you will lose again and you will lose you will lose.

The idleness of manipulation, what is done, and done for, and done in.

*

He can't say; he can't play; he can't delay   anymore.

*

It's more of the same, and isn't it always the same when fire plays with fire?

*

In anarchy is unrest and in unrest is the reckless, the hopeless, the fearless, the careless.

In the city of anarchy, in the veil of the city is the first of the city, the caricature of the city, the anxiety of the city is the first of the city, the origin of the city, the knowledge of the city, the beat of the city, the haze of the city, the sketch of the city, the temptation of the city, the menacing of the city, the dismissal of the city, the affluence of the city, the idealism of the city, the scapegoat of the city, the want of the city, the thirst of the city, the horror of the city, the crank of the city, the architect of the city, the people of the city, the people of the anarchy, the anarchy of the people

*

Listen, this is how it works, anarchy.
We fall in on ourselves.
We fall in on the city.
And the city falls in on us.

And the point is, the struggle is in the disarray; the common good is in
the anarchy. An arch.

You push back against it by being who you are.

Anarchy is derived from the word ánarchos, meaning "without a head or
chief, headless."
Headless.
Even headless,
Our city sees
With its eyes.
The disorder
Is ordered
Without.

I THREW IN AN EXTRA FUCK

I threw in an extra fuck because it's spring
I threw in an extra fuck because the long before is here
I threw in an extra fuck because the riveting scene is delivered
I threw in an extra fuck because this is grueling
I threw in an extra fuck because I have noted the exploits
I threw in an extra fuck because the shit is burgeoning
I threw in an extra fuck because the shit is rising
I threw in an extra fuck because i don't know what matters
I threw in an extra fuck because of courage
I threw in an extra fuck because tactics are rising in my throat
I threw in an extra fuck because I'm political
I threw in an extra fuck because why the fuck not?
I threw in an extra fuck because we need a new beginning
I threw in an extra fuck because of discrimination
I threw in an extra fuck because I have seen the luminaries
I threw in an extra fuck because I see you
I threw in an extra fuck because your curtain will soon be torn
I threw in an extra fuck because it isn't all hope and dreams
I threw in an extra fuck because sometimes language is ugly
I threw in an extra fuck because of my sympathy
I threw in an extra fuck because chance is brilliant
I threw in an extra fuck because victory is near
I threw in an extra fuck because the throat is remarkable
I threw in an extra fuck because it isn't all about what you say
I threw in an extra fuck because the tyrant only speaks bullshit

EVOLUTION HINGES ON ITS MISTAKES

I think about what falls away from us. I think about our greatest scares. What is our broader wonder, if not one that hinges on what we have left? This world that indicates *virtue,* sometimes likes to thrive in *vice.*

*

The language of the tyrant hinges on what makes us human. I will make this more accessible: think of legacy, think of its magnitude and then think of what surpasses history and time. Is it death? Is it memory? Is it what is written down, or is it what is implicit in our rage?

*

There are thorns in his wrapper. There are thrashes in his wreck.

When the Tyrant says, *I hereby demand,* it is already inevitable. He is already eclipsing the truth, shunning the light. All tyrants lack, but in their lack is their eternity. They all live on, despite their downfalls, in haunt and in forever-shadow.

*

There are thirsts in this worth, and in this fearing. Realize the rot is only getting larger. No one expected the testing of this; no one expected to raise humanity from a lie. No one expected the theft of his wreck, his craft-landing, this carving of light. We are expected to cramp, skewer, scram, skiff and skid, but remember, the biggest iris is you.

STAY QUIET

after it is announced that ICE Detains More Children at the Border *on June 22, 2018*

I'm on the 2 train to Penn Station, worn and worried, but bighearted and drawn-in. [This is the moment when you almost want to shake me, but you don't, because my feelings are shorthand for my hope.] On this day, everyone is thumbing their anger, and carelessly flipping off the quiet. [This is the moment when you almost want to pull me out of this scene, but you can't because the doors have just closed.] It is a surreal juxtaposition, an experiment in pettiness. I came in after. A man was yelling at a woman, *Do you know how I feel? Do you know how I feel?* To which the woman responded, *I said I was sorry. I didn't see you.* The man badgers on, *You stepped on me. You didn't feel that?* I look around. I am standing by the door. I feel the threat on my throat. I feel the brutality in my knees. [This is the moment when you want to tell me I'm being dramatic, and I am, but I feel it in my gut, in my spleen – that anger needs a bigger destination.] Suddenly, the gates of hell fly open, stubborn and raging. There are two small children, tourists I think, watching, hiding behind their mother at the door. Another man saddles out of his apathy with *she said she was sorry*, and the first man turns, like a thief, caught in a robbery, and I see his face go blank. He turns again to the woman, *what are you going to do about the children? What are you going to do about the children?* The story could end here, but sometimes the world goes red. Sometimes the world flails and burns. This is a larger mystery. I avert my gaze and look at the woman sitting closest to where I stand. She is on her cell phone reading what looks like The Bible *The lord fights so you can stay quiet* and I wish, for a second, that I had that kind of faith. Don't we all want to pick a fight with this world? *Stay quiet,* I mutter to no one. *Stay quiet,* I mutter to the door. *Stay quiet,* I mutter to the platform. *Stay quiet,* I mutter to my heart, *stay quiet.*

HATE DREAM

I dream hate. I dream fear. I barely remember my dreams but through the scrape of a night, I see the world is at my glass. No storms or blizzards could have prepared me for this hate, for this blur, for this telling of time. And me. While I. Me. Slept at a friend's place. Me. Wanted to be closer to work. Me. In dream, I desert my fear for a hot minute. Me. I deserted my sense of self. I deserted my people and my past. I heat my fear in my hands with my eyes. I see in this dream. I fear. I see the drawing of fire across my friend's window. I seethe. I scream. I cry. I, see the word HATE on the glass. Torrents spill from my mouth. I shock. I burn. I split. I flame. I cry. I try, through the dream, through my peripheral, through the windowpane, but narrow is my scream and narrow is my struggle, but not my truth. Not my strength. It never passes.

WHAT EVEN MATTERS ANYMORE

In the group memory of this time in our lives, of this year of the tyrant, what
Emerges: the collapse, the attack, the possessing of this utter nonsense? Even
The collective sees history case by case, marveling at who is turned away, at what matters.
We can't just say, I remember, and watch it pass; we can't forget anymore.

What I think about is this article on CNN, "How to Date in 2018" and my feelings themselves
Even leave me, threading together for another obstacle of this life, this passing. What
Matters now? I'm not sure, but the article talks about rehumanizing sex, and that doesn't kill me
Anymore because I see it, with my own eyes. I see the unnamable; I know this is grueling.

I think about what is vengeful or humorous, but in the end, I think of strength. What
World is this that we are slipping back through time? Rehumanize, as if we have even
Lost touch with our logic, our reasoning, our joie de vive. Well, no. Many have taken matters
Into their own hands, taking love out, taking consent out and everything else out. Not anymore,

Does the idea of love resonate? It is a fad, a treasure to be dug up even, and what
Am I supposed to say? What am I supposed to tell my future children about this, when even
The heart is viewed in scorn? I am human. I am alive with the beating of what matters.
I am not fearless. I fear, but I fear with my heart at my tongue. We can't yield anymore.

THE WILD ITSELF

Colors are a gift. —Zayan, age 5

Isn't it wild when you feel alone, but you are not alone and the greatest strength, the greatest cut is the one that is a graze, a smear, a stain, or how *kindness goes a long way*? It does and it does, and it does.

We all need one another, and our need is right there, beside you.

*

> My Lyft driver home from the airport said he didn't feel good and asked me if he should go to the hospital and where should he leave his car, and if it was alright if he dropped me at the corner.
>
> *Yes*, I said, and *go,* and *don't worry.*

I've been noticing the way the need saddles up; carrying its roots in one hand, begrudging, intuitive, intrusive, wild and holy, wildly holy, like it's pushing up and out of you: a sprout.

*

> On my way home from the 92nd St. Y, I poked my head down a taxi cab window to see if the driver was free; he nodded yes and unlocked the door, and I got in and he said, *can you wait a minute; I can't stand not throwing out garbage;* I said *sure* and he said *some people don't want to wait* and I said, *you mean you thought I would say no?* and he said, *some people do* and he asked what I did for a living, and I said I was a teacher and he said *teachers are my favorite people— they have to be patient* and I laughed. I couldn't believe that people say *no* and I asked *how long have*

you been a taxi driver and he said *20 years* and I asked *what is your favorite part* and he said, *the interesting people. Yes*, I thought, we are all so interesting, even those that are unkind, but the kind ones are the ones that make it worthwhile.

I have noticed the way the need suffers, in all lowercase, lolling its head from left to right, its face flushed red, then white, beside you—you needn't look far—it's on the periphery—if you only bend.

*

I got off the C train at 59th Street when it started to go express and when the next local came, a woman walked up to me and I thought *Why it is always me* but then I looked up at her. The train pulled up and she said, *Can I hold on to you when crossing the gap* and I said *what* and she said *I have vertigo and that feels like the world gone sideways* and so she very-gently, held my sleeve and stepped into the train car thanking me over and over again and I got off at 72nd street and she said *you have a nice day* and *happy holidays* and *thanks for helping me* and I looked at her kind face and her wild white hair and thought, *who wouldn't let her hold on?*

I've been noticing the way our need makes its home, like a delivery at our stoop; leaving a mark, a thread, a syllable, a tang, a thumbprint, a bruise; but we are more, and we are fond and...

*

And the gift,

Again, the gift

Again, the gift ends

Where the gift begins

Again, the gift is matter of fact

The gift is a place

The gift is behind

The gift is anguished

The gift is quiet

And desperate

And cruel

Again, the gift embarks

Again, the gift grouches

The gift slights

The gift is amused

The gift is desire

      and the desire turns: off

Again, the slouch

Again, the estimation

Again, the realm of the gift

The whale of the gift

The whole of the gift

The whirl of the gift

Its covering

Its uncovering

Again, the gift

Again, it's going

Again, it's away

again, it is here again in

the orb of moon   its halo   the fallen leaf   the crack of sun

the rose lining of cloud   the fire of sunset   the lemon of sunrise

this breath   this day,   this hour

this day   the color of it   all

MAKE IT

At the back of my feet, is winter
With its fragmented mash of would-be loathing.

The white light of consciousness, its hope, love, and despair
All engineer what I now realize: *what will pass, will pass.*

I cascade onto another street corner, drawing together
A following of moments, of struggles, of my newfound politics.

What is delivered in disruption, traffic, the cold, and my breath in the cold,
Turns into something vulnerable, something a single fear could swat away.

At the corner of Broadway and 64th street,
Racing to make the light, racing to widen my pace, my gaze, and my heart

I hear praise. I turn my head and a mother is carrying her child
Across the street saying, "you have been so good today," as she puts her

Down at the median. I smile. We all would like to hear those affirmations.
The second light turns green, and the numbers start descending, 25, 24, 23

I'm texting a friend. I see that same mother and daughter start to run
22, 21, 20. The mother has an open smile, compelling the length of her whole being

With song. 14, 12, 10. I hear the daughter start screaming, "We are going to make it!
We are going to make it!" Her mother takes her hand, as they step up on to the curb.

I look at them, and then I look at the light turn from 5 to 4 to 2 to 0. I think to myself
We are going to make it. I am going to make it. This day, this month. This year.

What perches, what roots, what winds and cracks
What tenses and dwells, what ails us, and what hurtles us down

Into the whistling air of despair, all will not stop us.
We are going to make it.

WOMAN ALIVE

And then I suddenly said, *it's good to be alive*
and I meant it, not in the way of the reckless
but in the way a ban is lifted and then wrecked.

I said, *it's good to be alive* because it is good
and in this offering of myself to you,
I am doused in the familiar,
something warm and soothing. It is merely
caricature to mention fainting
or smelling salts or worse, hyperbole.
I am currently *feeling*
so much more than the current state
of this horrible world.
It is good to be alive,
because I feel the coming of the tides,
because I feel the frill and the spray
and the shortening and widening of shores
with each of my openings.

If the sharp claws of the tyrant
find their way to my temple,
I am already gone,
in a pulse of beauty,
a stir of honesty,
a dance of lap and lip and bottom.
I, I, I, I, I am orchestrating this living,
heightening chords, flattening lows,
and sharpening myself into the ambient.

If the giant fangs of the tyrant
find the path to my pulse,
I am already infecting him
with my truth,
that I am ready to fall,

that I have already fallen,
that the falling was a leap I welcomed
and the only time I felt most like myself;
that the melancholy has passed,
that the gray-sea-water, I have been treading,
has sea-foamed and natured itself
into something fresh
and pulsing with organisms.

It is good to be alive under the tyrant,
for he highlights how we should love,
how we can make our own rules
how to remember that life can still surprise us
if we open ourselves to risk,
if we oyster our way out of hate,
and rage and stupor,
haphazardly and sideways,
swollen and pearled
with our pride,
with our pain
with our wants
and muscle ourselves
into willing.
For the only thing
stronger than the tyrant
is the heart.

WHAT YOU GIVE TO A THIEF IS STOLEN

after James Richardson

What chance & thrill it must be to resist this.
You love the thing of this, the hamstring of its desire, but
Give it over to the fight. Fight it hard & good. Love it, for it is easily taken, given over
To the wants of others, the bump up against tyranny. They are taking this from us:
A smile here, a rub there, a shared comfort. All the tenderings of our ways, see the
Thief. See the scene of their choreography. See the way they dance around the issue. It
Is an act of infliction & bedevilment. So many of our moments are taken without consent,
Stolen, labeled inconsequential. They cannot write this away. The power is always in words.

LOVE, TYRANT, LOVE

It is always related to love; how can it not be?
Love, Tyrant, Love.

DESIRE [EVEN IN THE TIME OF THE TYRANT]

then i am sprawling in through me
then i am fastened into myself
into my points and my pulls
then i am spinning in rev, in stare
it is a stun and a shunning of this life
it is a slutting of this life
it is a spawning of this moment
i am a promise awake with knowing
a pull in a thread
sprawling
a sputtering
a stuttering
a slant
a song
a rising
a falling
a driving to the edge & waiting
a waiting for the edge to fall
an edging closer to the fall
a wanting the fall to crush
and now i am in the fall
i am the fall
i thank the desire
i kiss the desire
i hold the desire
i thumb the desire
i bite the desire
i thrust the desire
i grind the desire
i rub the desire
it is without oars
& sitting
lulling
circling in a pond
it is the wind tracing

the feet of the kicking beneath that surface
the earth beneath sucking & sucking
that filling of the mouth
that shattering of time
i am bringing myself to a standstill
i am allowing the water to spread
i am afloat in the desire
the desire of me
of you
i am pinning myself to the surface
waiting for the moon to fall
longing for the pierce of stars
tonguing the night
brushing away the darkness
til there is light
around
beneath
inside
til my eyes
open
to the white
of the sky

SURRENDER

I'm trying to imagine a better future.   I'm trying to imagine

my grace like a finger pulling me   my grace

like a natural tugging   imagine that

my trying to cure and current, wrangle and love

trying to find: calm

in knowing I'm not fooling around.

               in knowing I'm working and working and working and working

I know desire has an element of fear. I know that fear

has an element of attraction   see

see   see   the way this is spooling.

f e e l   the untethering at my ankle   at my hip

at my tongue

               I get that I need to live in this, if I want this if I want if I'm wanting

I know, I'm not fooling around.   I'm trying to imagine

stillness stilling,   a stolen silence

captured, seized, or a taking refuge in the breath   t h i s

Trying to find: patience

in knowing I'm not fooling around, but I'm at the cusp, risking

               in knowing   I'm in this I'm in this I'm in this

I know all of life is a loop. I know that turning, I know that turn

that turn   has an element of fight, but a curve cannot   go straight

a curve cannot heighten its low   f e e l

the untethering of these rules, of these days

be in the moment   Any one will say: pause

Trying to find: breath

In knowing I'm not fooling around.

                    In knowing, this is what this may look like

                    this is what this may look like

                    this is what this may look like

okay

okay

okay

okay

I know what this is

It's okay   to let it breathe   to breathe

this is how I surrender   I write my way through this moment

I follow the tug and the finger   I imagine the grace the willing took

remember the grace   and the willing

it is how I will explain this   to myself

      the willing

everything that happens in the world happens to us

I'm at my own center.

      Anyone will say: b r e a t h e

[OF] TYRANT IN JEST

Any
Rant
Any
Tat
Any
Ratatatat
Any
Tar Ant
Any
Nay
Any
Tan-Tart
Any
Ranttttttttttttttttttttttttttttttttttttttttttttttttttt
Rat

Rat

Rat

Rat

RISE AND FALL OF THE TYRANT

I.

There are so many tyrants around us   where the heartache is

the treachery   the fragility   the suggesting

the activating   we hallucinate   we house our anger

          we sting the teeming   but obsession overcomes us

like raw flesh   it burns::vibrates::hums   all desire nerves away

                     all kindness perishes

[The tyrant is everywhere, and one must consider the price of freedom]

The tyrant is at your job

The tyrant follows you home

The tyrant is in your grief

The tyrant is in your longing

The tyrant is in your sick

The tyrant is in your heart

The tyrant is on your train

The tyrant is beneath your earnesty

The tyrant is in your breath

The tyrant is in this poem

II.

She, herself
She, offering
she, she, she, she, she
She tells me
She wishes he would hit her
She tells me
No one has spoken to her like this before
She tells me
The shape
Of his wounds
Of his rage
Of his childness
Of his impossibility
Of his stupor
Of his prickliness
She tells me
She is the destination
Of his anger
Unreasonable
Irrational
Demented
She tells me
She is too strong
She tells me
It is her fault for taking it
I tell her

The tyrant is everywhere

I tell her

She isn't taking it

She doesn't believe him

She is just absorbing

Yes, it is maddening

Yes, it is ungodly

Yes, it is unbearable

But he will be taken down

They all will

III.

What

World

What

Scab

What

Voice

Stimulates

Him?

What

Sanity

What

Unraveling

What

Mingling

Seizes

Him?

What

Rulings
What
Justice
What
Rush
Civilizes
Him?

IV.

I would set fire
To this world
To this life
I would set fire
To these faults
If it meant
The tyrant
Would fall
It if meant
This world
Was not this world
If it meant
This world
Was not
A plaything.
What I want
What I want
More than anything
Is for the tyrant
To leave

Is for the tyrant
To leave my hand
Is for the tyrant
To leave my grip
For the tyrant
To remove
His fangs
From my palm
Is for the tyrant
To let me
Rise
Rise
Rise
Is for the tyrant
To let me rise
From the lonely
Alone.

TENDER

I think about the word: TENDER
And its meanings
He told me I was so tender
Tender meaning easily to bruise?
Meaning soft to the touch?
Meaning perfection to taste?
Meaning juicy
Or close to bloody
Tender...
Did he mean *tinder*?
Like when I saw him on Tinder
Like when I saw someone who *might've* been posing as him on Tinder?
Or like what starts a fire?
The way the wood balks
The way it bleeds blue into orange into yellow
(Orange you glad I never called you out about that?)
Doesn't the wood grow warm and gentle, soft-like?
(One might say *tender)*
Was he saying I was quick to burn?
(Maybe he was quick to burn)
Maybe I am quick to burn
(So what?)
Tender feels so loving
All those "en" sounds like envelope endearment endeavor
encircle enclose enchant entwine enthral engage
end end end end end end end end end end end end end

TORPOR

Monster comes from the Latin verb: *monstrare* meaning "to show"
And the Latin verb *monare* meaning "to warn."

What are they showing or warning when they stand before us in the flesh?

Monsters used to entertain, not fear, not scare,
But now, they give shape to the aura, to nightmare, to despair

Monsters define us.

There is always a snake in a supporting role, defining the sin from the sinner.
There is always a maddening move between fear and anxiety, from anxiety to terror.

Monsters enhanced the aura of those in power.

What about the one in power now? His sickening resonance.
His political scheme. What mistake, trauma or grief can he drain now?   Or now?

Did you know Hummingbirds can enter a state of torpor to conserve energy to stay alive?

After lowering its heartbeat and using just enough energy, it needs to kickstart its entire being.
What sounds like snoring is a gasping for air, a gush of the vocal cords. All things gasp.

What is our survival strategy?
How do I shutdown this anger, smolder this rage?

How do I conserve, diminish, reserve, preserve, reuse this energy inside me,
As to unfathom my fear, as to fracture the lies of this world, and revive the heart gone torpor.

MARVEL [AT WOMAN] OR WOMAN: LAST MONSTE

It is like being the alien within the alien,
living the everyday instances of anger.
Sometimes monster,
sometimes battling   or baffling.
Whatever snarls, whatever guilts,
whatever heralds into new lands
is a conundrum,
is a mystery:
sphinxated.

*

A. Sphinx = *woman combining masculine intellect &*
feminine sexuality.

B. Sphinx = Monster

———————————

∴ Woman = Monster

*

What kind of monster is woman? What kind of monster is a woman
who demonstrates her demons; who demonstrates her exoticisms; who
demonstrates her intelligence, and her tender? What kind of monster
is part puzzle part breast, part mystery part best?

It is a sacred hunt being woman between being heat and heart. We
marvel, yet we are marveled at. We are the marveled and the marvel
itself. We marvel at the world as it is and we marvel at the way we are
not; at the way we are *not* man; at the way we are *not* stone or sand
or sea; at the way we are not even seen; at the way our own soft is not
our own, nor our own disruption, or nature. Even our wonder is not
wondered at.

Our breath is trickery; our eyes deception; our touch sheer-hypocrisy; our tongue a worm; our thighs, a length to measure what spawn. Our trickery is in our might; our trickery is in our flight; our trickery is in the power between us; the power between our lips; the power between our eyes; the power between our breasts.

Your destruction is in your foolery; Your destruction is in your own trickery; your destruction is in your insistence. Your trickery is in your stubbornness; your trickery is in your firm, your hand, your steeled; your trickery brings about your destruction; Your stupidity brings about our devouring.

In our riddle, is the way we live. In our riddle, is the we walk this life sunlit; In our riddle, is the we walk this life unscathed.

SELF-REFLECTION

1.

Apparently, St. Margaret was so pious that she was indigestible when the dragon tried to swallow her. The dragon didn't want her, was repelled by her, and saw her as alien. She was both easy to resist, yet also irresistible. It often feels like I am of the same flock. I repel; I reject; I shun; I halt; I discard; I deter; I resist, and I disavow.

2.

Inside is the alien / inside is the hunt / the hunt that makes monsters out of us / the hunt that makes us hunt the want / the hunt that makes the want / the hunt that makes us want the want / the hunt that makes us want the want that we want.

3.

My friend says, *you are different; you walked through the fire and came out the other side.*

//

I think about that fire. All my phoenixing. All my aligning and redefining. I think about all my reframing, all my scaffolding and my lexiconic leaps. What are they for? To establish *this* monstrosity? To establish *my* monstrosity? To establish the reflection of myself to myself?

//

In myself, I see the hope. I see the urgency. I also see the bleak. I see the way I reinforce this to myself, tearing the edges, punching the holes; I see the way I keep, and I hold and I stare, and I see the way this *should* go, and I see the way this *would* go, and then I see the way it *actually* is. In my own self is what is alien: the woman I've become, the woman I now am and the woman I thought I'd be. Who is to say any of us are better than any one of us? Who is to say we aren't all the same woman, for what woman is ever the same?

(Okay, let me stop dramatizing.)

4.

What I know is that I'm tired of fire, its heat and its staunch, its climb, its origin, and its sanctimony, its necessity, its ritual, its height, its spit and sear.

What I know is that I'm tired of looking *at* myself. I'm tired of looking *within* myself. I'm tired of looking *around* myself. I'm tired of looking *at* you in relation to me. I'm tired of looking at *this* in relation to me. I'm tired of looking. I'm tired of sifting and treading *oh so lightly*. In an instant, it *is* you. We are all of this now, of this tyrant. In an instant, nothing is bolstered, and everything is let loose.

ALTERNATE ENDING OF THE TYRANT

In an alternate ending of *King Lear*, written after Shakespeare's death, Cordelia dies in her father's arms and then Lear is hanged. No rights are wronged; no savior is found. Wrong begets wrong. Betrayal begets betrayal. In an alternate ending of *this* life, the tyrant falls in a swift, a swoop, a spoon's width away from comedy. In this ending, the tyrant gradually falls to pieces; circuits fail, edges crack, and hinges bust; the tyrant frails, his hands are already taken; in one hand lies all the evil deeds and in the other, all the cries of the people. All the Americans; all of those people he tried to separate, nullify, procure; all of those beautiful people he mined against one another, who he propped up with his puppetry and from whom he mystified the truth, those are the ones leading the fray. Lie by lie, layer by layer, the tyrant falls to the earth, and there is no burial song, no choir leading the audience in prayer; death is death. It is a certainty—we all die—and here, the tyrant is without his hands, and here, he is now without his tongue, without his voice, and without his hearing; he falls and falls and falls; no one pities him and no one cries. In this alternate ending, the need to feel fades; victory triumphs, freedom triumphs, peace triumphs, love triumphs; in this alternate ending, his ashes become a stone and the stone is buried in the dirt, captured in the dank and the dark and in the damp of eternity. The tyrant is just that, a pebble beneath the surface: one we *know* is always there, always there, *always*—

STUN

Every day I try to trust in the world, but I don't know where
my trust goes; the world is your toolbox, yet the world is your
tool. Dena makes a pagan mezuzah out of flowers for a friend
and tells me, someday, I'll make you one, and I think, how lovely,
and yes, but even without a mark, I'm a dead-giveaway. I'm a given.
There is such violence, such forgetting, and such holding on. The Tyrant
is thriving here, deep in these riches. THIS is his hellscape, his want,
I think, until my dentist asks how I'm feeling, and I say, conflicted; I say, still
processing, but it is not enough. (He laughs at that). It's NOT enough. There is
no sunny side of the street, though I'm looking. I don't want to pick
sides; I am for what's humane, yet, again, he asks about my feelings, my
Jewishness and says, even someone Reform, like you, would be taken out
in the street and massacred, and I am stunned, by the prick of his probe, the prick
of his honesty. Jew to Jew: the brutality stuns. The violence is everywhere.

TYRANT AS SELF REFLECTION

The tyrant sees himself when *he* sees you. He sees himself when he sees *you*. He *sees* himself when he sees *you*. Himself. *You*. Himself. *You*. Himself. *You*. Himself. Y*ou*. Himself. Y*ou*. Himself. The tyrant lives in the tyranny of *you*. The tyrant lives in the country of *you*. The tyrant lives in the y*ou*, in you. The you that the tyrant brings out, is the tyrant's *version* of you. The tyrant lives in the *you* he sees in himself. In the you he *sees*. In the you *he* sees. In the *you* he sees in you. In the you that is *not* you. In the you that is *him*. His outrage lies in your control. When the tyrant sees *your* control, he sees the control *he* desires. When the tyrant sees *your* love, he sees the love *he* desires. When the tyrant sees *your* love, he sees *his* love. When the tyrant sees *your* love, he *doesn't* see love, he doesn't *see* love, he *sees* himself. He sees the love he desires *for* himself. He sees the love he desires for *himself*. He sees the love he desires to feel. He sees his *own* love. He sees his self-love; he sees his reflection in *your* love. When the tyrant splits, he doesn't split for you, he splits to *better* himself. He splits into two, for two of him is better than one. He splits into two to see two reflections of *his* beautiful self. He sees himself butterflied. He sees the mirror of his beauty duplicated. The mirror of his beauty *is* the mirror of his lies. The mirror of his truth and his want. He *sees* the mirror and the way *out* of the mirror. He sees the mirror and he sees *you*, but the *you* he sees is himself. He sees himself, his self, his self *and* his self-reflection. His authority, his charisma, his availability and his cooing are all ways he attracts himself to himself, like a moth to a flame. In his attraction is *his* attraction to you. In his attraction is his *attraction* to you. He is attracted to you because he sees his own self-reflection in *your* truth, in *your* confidence, in *your* talent. When the tyrant says he is going to hurt you, he *is* going to hurt you, he is *going to* hurt you, *he* is going to hurt you, but he is *also* going to hurt himself. When the tyrant hurts you, he hurts himself. When he hurts *you,* he hurts himself, but in *your* hurt, he only sees his *own* hurt and, in *his* hurt, he sees himself and *not* you. When the Tyrant sees *you,* he sees himself. He *sees* you, but *mostly* sees himself. He sees himself. He sees himself *in* you. He sees *him* in you. He sees and sees and sees, but *only* sees himself. He sees your hands on him and he sees *his* hands on you. In his hands, he sees his hands, but he doesn't see them holding you. He sees *himself* in his hands. He sees himself holding himself. And when you cry, the tyrant hears his *own* cry. He wants to match your cry with *his* cry because in *your* cry is the tyrant's cry. In *your* cry, is the *more* beautiful cry and that is the cry of the tyrant, his reflection. In your cry, is the reflection of himself. In your cry, in your release, in your orgasm is the letting go that *he* desires. Y*our* letting go, makes him lose control. He sees *his* letting go in yours, but he also sees the control *you* lack and in *your* lack is *his* lack and in *your* lack, he sees *his* lack, and in *your* lack, he sees himself. *In you, he sees himself.* In your admiration, is his admiration. In your admiration, is his own admiration of *himself.* In your rise, is the tyrant's rise. In your fall, is the tyrant's fall. In your buckling is his buckling. In your wetness is the wetness he wishes *he* had. In your secrets, are his secrets. In your willing, is *his* willing. In your tease, is his tease. In you, the tyrant sees himself. He sees his platform, his hope, his fear, his solidarity and his piousness. In *you*, he sees himself atomized. In you, he sees his fears denounced. In *your* happiness, he sees *his* happiness, and the happiness he *could* have if he didn't see *his* lack. In *your* victories, his own victories. In *your* goodness, his own goodness, and his *own* goodness in you. He sees his *own* creativity, his *own* mechanisms turning, and his own mechanisms turning *in* you. In you, he sees his own buttress of rules landsliding. In his landslide, he sees *your* lack and in *your* lack is *his* lack. In affecting you, he is affecting himself. In accommodating you, he is accommodating himself. In working on himself, he is *only* working on himself, he is only working *on* himself, he is only working on *his self. His self.* In working on himself, he is manipulating himself, he is mastering himself to his self; he is mounting himself, look, he is mouthing something to his self: *I am you; I am the tyrant.*

NOTES

"I Want to Wear the Crown" is for Michael Roper.

"[Of Men]" is for Ruth Awad and Adam J. Gellings.

"I Threw in an Extra Fuck" is for Virginia Konchan.

"The Wild Itself" is for Zayan, Faisal and Hina.

"What Even Matters Anymore" owes a debt to Saturday Night Live
and Jessica Chastain's skit of the same name.

"Rise and Fall of the Tyrant" is for Heather Marshall.

"Alternate Ending of the Tyrant" owes a debt to Shakespeare's *King Lear*
and *Twelfth Night*.

"Tyrant As Self Reflection" owes a debt to Nancy Nereo.

Some of these poems were inspired by the exhibit "Medieval Monsters:
Terrors, Aliens, Wonders" at The Morgan Library in NYC in 2018.

The title of this book was inspired by reading an excerpt of *The Federalist
Papers* and Margaret Atwood's *The Handmaid's Tale*.

ABOUT THE AUTHOR

Leah Umansky is also the author of two other full-length collections of poetry, *The Barbarous Century* and *Domestic Uncertainties*, and two chapbooks, *Straight Away the Emptied World* and the Mad-Men inspired *Don Dreams and I Dream*.

Umansky earned her MFA in Poetry at Sarah Lawrence College and has curated and hosted The COUPLET Reading Series in NYC since 2011. Her creative work can be found in *The New York Times*, The Academy of American Poets' *Poem-A-Day*, *USA Today*, *POETRY*, and *American Poetry Review*.

She has taught workshops to writers of all ages in such places as The Poetry School (UK), Hudson Valley Writers Center, and Memorial Sloan Kettering's *Visible Ink* Program.

ABOUT THE WORD WORKS

Since its founding in 1974, The Word Works has steadily published volumes of contemporary poetry and presented public programs. Its imprints include The Washington Prize, The Tenth Gate Prize, The Hilary Tham Capital Collection, and International Editions.

Monthly, The Word Works offers free programs in its Café Muse Literary Salon. Starting in 2023, the winners of the Jacklyn Potter Young Poets Competition will be presented in the June Café Muse program.

As a 501(c)3 organization, The Word Works has received awards from the National Endowment for the Arts, the National Endowment for the Humanities, the D.C. Commission on the Arts & Humanities, the Witter Bynner Foundation, Poets & Writers, The Writer's Center, Bell Atlantic, the David G. Taft Foundation, and others, including many generous private patrons.

An archive of artistic and administrative materials in the Washington Writing Archive is housed in the George Washington University Gelman Library. The Word Works is a member of the Community of Literary Magazines and Presses and its books are distributed by Small Press Distribution.

wordworksbooks.org

OTHER WORD WORKS BOOKS

Annik Adey-Babinski, *Okay Cool No Smoking Love Pony*
Karren L. Alenier, *From the Belly: Poets Respond to Gerturude Stein's* Tender Buttons
Karren L. Alenier, *Wandering on the Outside*
Emily August, *The Punishments Must Be a School*
Jennifer Barber, *The Sliding Boat Our Bodies Made*
Carrie Bennett, *The Land Is a Painted Thing*
Rachel Bennett, *Mothers & Other Fairy Tales*
Andrea Carter Brown, *September 12*
Willa Carroll, *Nerve Chorus*
Grace Cavalieri, *Creature Comforts | The Long Game: Poems Selected & New*
Abby Chew, *A Bear Approaches from the Sky*
Nadia Colburn, *The High Shelf*
Henry Crawford, *Binary Planet*
Barbara Goldberg, *Berta Broadfoot and Pepin the Short*
          | Breaking & Entering: New and Selected Poems
Akua Lezli Hope, *Them Gone*
Michael Klein, *The Early Minutes of Without: Poems Selected & New*
Deborah Kuan, *Women on the Moon*
Frannie Lindsay, *If Mercy*
Elaine Magarrell, *The Madness of Chefs*
Chloe Martinez, *Ten Thousand Selves*
Marilyn McCabe, *Glass Factory*
JoAnne McFarland, *Identifying the Body*
Leslie McGrath, *Feminists Are Passing from Our Lives*
Kevin McLellan, *Ornitheology*
Ron Mohring, *The Boy Who Reads in the Trees*
A. Molotkov, *Future Symptoms*
Ann Pelletier, *Letter That Never*
W.T. Pfefferle, *My Coolest Shirt*
Ayaz Pirani, *Happy You Are Here*
Robert Sargent, *Aspects of a Southern Story | A Woman from Memphis*
Roger Smith, *Radiation Machine Gun Funk*
Jeddie Sophonius, *Love & Sambal*
Julia Story, *Spinster for Hire*
Barbara Ungar, *Naming the Animals*
Cheryl Clark Vermeulen, *They Can Take It Out*
Julie Marie Wade, *Skirted*
Miles Waggener, *Superstition Freeway*
Fritz Ward, *Tsunami Diorama*
Camille-Yvette Welsch, *The Four Ugliest Children in Christendom*
Amber West, *Hen & God*
Maceo Whitaker, *Narco Farm*

www.ingramcontent.com/pod-product-compliance
Lightning Source LLC
Chambersburg PA
CBHW031930080426
42734CB00007B/626